ISAAC ASIMOV'S
Library of the Universe

Unidentified Flying Objects

by Isaac Asimov

Gareth Stevens Publishing
Milwaukee

Library of Congress Cataloging-in-Publication Data

Asimov, Isaac, 1920-
  Unidentified flying objects.

  (Isaac Asimov's library of the universe)
  Bibliography: p.
  Includes index.
  Summary: Briefly discusses facts and fantasies about UFOs.
  1. Unidentified flying objects -- Juvenile literature. [1. Unidentified flying objects] I. Title. II. Series: Asimov, Isaac, 1920-   . Library of the universe.
TL789.A75   1988   001.9'42   87-42604
ISBN 1-55532-355-3 (lib. bdg.)
ISBN 1-55532-380-4

A Gareth Stevens Children's Books edition

Edited, designed, and produced by
Gareth Stevens, Inc.   7317 West Green Tree Road   Milwaukee, Wisconsin 53223, USA

Cover photography and artwork © Julian Baum 1988
Designer: Laurie Shock
Picture research: Kathy Keller
Artwork commissioning: Kathy Keller and Laurie Shock
Project editor: Mark Sachner
Research editor: Scott Enk
Technical advisers and consulting editors: Julian Baum, Tom Pelnar, Francis Reddy, and Greg Walz-Chojnacki

    3 4 5 6 7 8 9 94 93 92 91 90 89

Printed in the United States of America

CONTENTS

Nowadays, we have seen planets up close, all the way to distant Uranus. We have mapped Venus through its clouds. We have seen dead volcanoes on Mars and live ones on Io, Jupiter's satellite. We have detected strange objects no one knew anything about until recently: quasars, pulsars, black holes. We have learned amazing facts about how the Universe was born and have some ideas about how it may die. Nothing can be more astonishing and more interesting.

But that doesn't mean we have solved everything about the Universe. There are puzzles that remain. Many are puzzles only to astronomers at their instruments as they wonder about objects they see millions of light-years away. But some puzzles are close to home and interest the general public. What about strange lights in the sky we sometimes see? These are unidentified flying objects, or UFOs.

What can they possibly be?

Isaac Asimov

Are UFOs for Real?

People <u>do</u> see strange objects in the sky they can't explain. Because these objects are in the sky, they are "flying." Because they don't seem to be explainable, they are "unidentified."

The present-day UFO excitement started in 1947, when pilot Kenneth Arnold saw a formation of bright circular objects skimming the mountaintops. He later described them as looking like saucers skipping across water. The name "flying saucers" caught on. But there are other UFOs. Some go very far back in time, and not all look like saucers.

Kenneth Arnold saw something from his plane that day in 1947.

Flying saucers — fact or fancy? Here's how one might look to earthlings on an otherwise uneventful family outing.

UFOs of the Past

Hundreds, even thousands, of years ago, what did people think about when they looked at the sky and saw things they could not explain? We can't always be sure. But one thing we <u>do</u> know: Today, even ancient stories remind some people of UFOs!

According to the Bible, Elijah was carried up to heaven in a fiery chariot, and Ezekiel reported seeing such a chariot. Vague stories and legends have come to us for centuries. In the 1500s, for instance, people reported seeing spheres and disks in the sky over Germany and Switzerland.

August 7, 1566: According to reports, a group of round objects appeared in the sky over Basel, Switzerland, and raced toward the Sun. Before vanishing, some turned toward each other, as if in combat.

With a little imagination, we might picture Ezekiel's "wheels" vision as a scene in a science fiction movie.

Ezekiel's vision — UFOs in the Bible?

In the first chapter of the Book of Ezekiel, the prophet Ezekiel tells of a vision he saw. It is very hard to understand, but he tells of four humanlike creatures, each with four faces and four wings, and each with hooves. What's more, they were accompanied by wheels within wheels that moved with them, and as the whole thing moved, there was a great noise. What did Ezekiel see? Should we conclude that the Book of Ezekiel reports a UFO sighting?

In 1896 people began reporting cigar-shaped objects that looked like airships. A rash of such reports came from England and New Zealand between 1909 and 1913. Soon reports poured in from many countries.

World War II "foo-fighters": Like mascots following their team out onto the playing field, these strange disks and spheres reportedly followed US aircraft on bombing missions over Europe. Sightings of foo-fighters were reported on several occasions, and their origin remains a mystery to this day.

The Great Pyramid — built by an alien stonecutter?

In about 2500 BC, the ancient Egyptians built the Great Pyramid, which is made up of about 2,300,000 blocks of stone each weighing thousands of pounds. No one knows exactly how the Egyptians could have built such a mighty structure with their simple tools. Some people think that aliens from UFOs in the far past built the pyramid. But others ask instead why such aliens would not have built even <u>one</u> item out of a more advanced material than stone.

Seen from the air, these lines near Nazca, Peru, often trace familiar patterns, such as this hummingbird (left picture). Some think the lines might be runways for vehicles from other worlds. It's more likely, however, that they are roads built around AD 900 — by earthlings — for special ceremonies.

UFOs Today

So people have been seeing brightly lit things in the skies for ages. Sometimes, though, they report something other than strange lights. Because we send up "flying objects" of our own, such as airplanes, missiles, balloons, and spacecraft, it is easy to think that UFOs may be advanced vehicles of some sort.

Some people report feeling heat, static electricity, sickness, or other unusual things in the area of the vehicles, which they describe in detail.

So what is true and what is imaginary? Unfortunately, it's hard to know just from the stories people tell.

Sometimes our imaginations make us think "flying saucer" when all we're really seeing is a "flying object." What do the objects in these pictures, one taken in Hawaii (right) and the other in Peru (below), look like to you?

In the mid-1980s, several police officers saw something in the sky near Belleville, Wisconsin. Although radar tracked the object, no one has been able to explain what it was. This picture was taken in Belleville, and the UFO has been added by an artist to give you an idea of what the people saw.

Repeat Performances

I find it hard to believe that UFO sightings can really be flying ships. There have been thousands of reports, but nothing in the way of solid evidence. You might think that with all those ships flying about, at least one would have crashed or dropped something! There have been photographs, of course, but they are not very clear.

Then, too, whenever a really sensational sighting is reported, there are suddenly dozens of other reports. Some UFO groups argue that these additional sightings confirm the first. And they say a UFO announcement may encourage people to come forward with sightings they had been afraid to report earlier.

But people often imitate each other, and fads that grab millions of people can fade overnight. And none of these stories has produced any real evidence that says, "<u>This</u> came from a UFO!"

Cradle Hill, in Warminster, Wiltshire, England: As the scene of several repeat performances, Cradle Hill was known as a UFO "hot spot" in the 1960s.

Above: High-altitude lenticular, or lens-shaped, clouds can play tricks on your eyes.

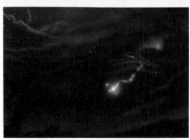

Ball lightning (above) and weather balloons (right) are unfamiliar sights to most of us.

Natural Phenomena

There is no doubt that people sometimes see things in the sky they don't understand. Many things — meteor trails, or the planet Venus, or comets, or odd-shaped clouds, or ball lightning, or the burning of marsh gases (known as "will o' the wisp"), even moving airplanes or the lights of distant cars — can seem mysterious.

Then, too, since scientists don't understand everything, there may be lights in the sky for reasons that we don't understand — at least not yet. There is nothing wrong in reporting such things.

July 16, 1969: While on their way to becoming the first crew to land humans on the Moon, the Apollo 11 astronauts spotted this strange object. The US government has identified it as a piece of space "junk" from Apollo's Saturn rocket. Other people aren't so sure. What does it look like to you?

Control tower to Venus: "You're cleared to land!"

UFO investigator Allan Hendry told this amusing story on "The Case of the UFOs" — a "NOVA" episode about the accuracy of UFO sightings. Air traffic controllers in a busy airport were expecting the arrival of a flight in the eastern sky during dawn hours. When they spotted Venus out the control tower window, they radioed the planet clearance to land! Hendry says this goes to show that "even the best-trained observers can be fooled by this unusually bright planet."

Faking It — Do-it-yourself UFOs

Unfortunately, some people like to get their names in the papers, or have fun fooling people. It is easy to take a picture of a spaceship model so it looks as if it is floating in the sky. People can also fake rows of lights. Sometimes, people make fake UFO pictures by just keeping the camera out of focus, or putting a drop of developer on the negative. Some hoaxers are quite skilled at making fake photographs.

Many of these hoaxes have been investigated and dismissed. And the more hoaxes there are, the more difficult it is to believe any of the reports, and the more skeptical many investigators get.

Would <u>you</u> be fooled by this fake UFO photo (left)? Not if you saw the whole picture! All it took to create this fake UFO was a camera, two paper-plate bowls stapled together, a felt marker, and a partner in crime to throw the "flying saucer."

The man with the telescope is a UFO hoaxer. His "Venusian flying saucer" (below) is a fake. It actually looks a lot like a chicken brooder — available by mail right here on Earth!

Invasion from Mars!

In 1938, actor and writer Orson Welles broadcast a radio drama of H. G. Wells' War of the Worlds. In it, "news bulletins" said that Martian ships were attacking in New Jersey, then spreading over the US. Welles had clearly said, "This is not truth. It is fiction," and no astronomers at the time believed there was advanced life on Mars. But just the same, many believed the story, and crowds of people in New Jersey got into their cars and fled in panic.

Two of the most famous "saucer" shots around, each taken by Paul Trent in Oregon on the evening of May 11, 1950. The large picture shows an object sailing over a tool shed and utility pole in the Trents' back yard. The smaller picture (inset) is an enlarged detail of the same UFO.

Visitors from Space?

Perhaps the most popular explanation of UFOs is that they are not only ships, but alien ships with creatures from other worlds aboard.

We understand enough about our Solar system today to know that if there are aliens in outer space, they must live on worlds many light-years away. The trip from their world to our world would have to be difficult and would take incredible amounts of energy, dedication, and sacrifice.

"It was very bright . . . and there was no noise or smoke," Mr. Trent said of the saucer. Added Mrs. Trent, "It was shiny but not as bright as a hubcap . . . and awfully pretty."

Right: another famous "saucer," this one photographed by a magazine photographer on May 7, 1952, as it flew over a Brazilian coastal city.

The Trindade Island sighting, January 16, 1958. Taken by an official photographer of the Brazilian Navy, this photo has raised many questions. Even though the photographer was known for his trick photography, the Brazilian Navy has vouched for its accuracy.

It is unlikely that our advanced instruments would <u>not</u> detect a major expedition traveling great distances from another star. It is even more unlikely that a <u>fleet</u> of so many different shapes and sizes would be able to buzz our planet for 40 years or more without being identified.

UFO Kidnappings: Are They for Real?

No attempt by any alien ship to make official contact with authorities on Earth has been reported. Yet a number of people not only have seen such alien ships, they say, but have also boarded those ships and seen the aliens themselves.

But in every case, all we have is a story. Some descriptions of the ships, the instruments on board, and the aliens themselves seem to be copied from science fiction books and movies! What's more, the people who say they have been on board these ships never bring back anything material — a button, a sheet of paper, <u>anything</u> that can be seen to be of alien origin.

Some of these reports are undoubtedly hoaxes. Others, however, are made by people who believe sincerely in their experiences. But in the eyes of the public, people's sincere beliefs often count for nothing in the absence of concrete evidence.

Right: Howard Menger — UFO abductee? He holds a "free-energy motor" built, he reports, under the direction of space people.

Below: Alan Godfrey also claims to have been abducted by a UFO. Here he tells his story, complete with artwork.

An assortment of humanoid space aliens. Each drawing is based on a description given by a person who claims to have been kidnapped by beings from outer space. Can you pick out the ways in which they are similar?

Government Investigations —
UFO Busters vs. UFO Believers

Many people think we should check out reports of UFO sightings with great care. And indeed, many reported sightings are of interest to governments all over the world. After all, UFOs just might be advanced aircraft developed by unfriendly nations for unfriendly purposes.

Government investigations almost always conclude that there is nothing to the reports, that some have natural explanations, some are hoaxes, and some are just the result of panic or fear. Many people accept these conclusions. Others — such as J. Allen Hynek, an astronomer who once investigated UFO reports for the US government — feel that government investigations are not as thorough or honest as they might be. And still others — mainly those who believe UFOs are alien vehicles — simply refuse to accept such conclusions. They think the government is lying and hiding evidence.

Still, there are thousands of reports of UFO sightings. Are <u>all</u> of them wrong? Or are <u>all</u> the governments lying? It's hard to find the truth. But remember: Right now, scientists feel that there is no real <u>proof</u> that flying saucers exist.

J. Allen Hynek, UFO researcher. Even as a skeptic, he felt the US government had not done enough to investigate UFO sightings.

Mysterious circles in the corn at the Devil's Punchbowl, Cheesefoot Head, Hampshire, England. One day the smaller circle appeared, and two days later, the larger one appeared.

The Roswell Incident: If sheep could talk, the tales they might tell! When a rancher in New Mexico heard a crash during a storm late one night and found his land littered with debris the next morning, many people figured it must have been a crashed saucer! This painting shows what the rancher might have imagined was going on outside his window that stormy night.

When is a UFO <u>not</u> an unidentified flying object? — When someone identifies it!

There are many sensational books about UFOs. One book, The Roswell Incident, *tells of a flying saucer crash just two weeks after Kenneth Arnold's sighting in 1947. A rancher in New Mexico had found debris that seemed to have come from a crashed saucer. But a closer look at the evidence and a check with the US Air Force revealed the truth. The debris was from a crashed radar balloon, and it had, in fact, been found 10 days <u>before</u> Arnold's sighting.* ●

A Controversy Both New and Old

Despite the absence of strong evidence, many people accept UFOs as alien spaceships. For one thing, all the excitement is sensational, and some people like to believe sensational things.

Some people also believe everything they read in newspapers and magazines.

For example, in 1835, the New York *Sun* reported that a new and powerful telescope had discovered living creatures on the Moon. In fact, the report was a clever hoax by writer Richard A. Locke. Scientists already believed the Moon had neither air nor water. But thousands believed Locke's hoax, and for a while the *Sun* sold more newspapers than any paper in the world!

It's easy to start a rumor, and it's easy to fool people. After all, whenever someone announces that the world will come to an end on some particular day, many thousands believe. So sensational reports about UFOs will continue, and so will the controversy — no matter what!

Dinosaurs, elephants, and farmers beware — alien spaceships are out to get you. Read all about it!

The end of the world!

In the early 1800s, an American preacher named William Miller studied the Bible and concluded that the world would come to an end no later than March 1844. Thousands of people believed him. Many sold all their possessions and, dressed in white robes, waited on a hilltop to be snatched to heaven. Nothing happened. Miller said he had made a mistake and predicted a new day: October 22, 1844. Again, crowds waited. And again, guess what? Nothing happened.

Life on Other Worlds?

But isn't it possible that there is life on other worlds?

Yes, of course. After all, there are 200 billion stars in our Galaxy and at least 100 billion other galaxies. Among all those stars, a great many must be like the Sun and have planets like Earth. Perhaps millions of Earth-like planets have intelligent life forms!

But are they visiting us? The nearest such life forms are likely to be hundreds of light-years away at the very least. So even at the speed of light (which is the fastest possible), it would take them many hundreds of years to reach us.

One astronomer, J. Allen Hynek, thought there might be something to UFO sightings. He investigated 10,000 sightings and felt that about 500 could not be explained by known causes. By the time he died in 1986, however, he still had not been able to find any scientific facts that would have made him believe in alien vehicles.

Perhaps we, too, would like to think that some UFOs carry visitors from distant worlds. But until the facts can convince serious investigators, it's probably best to admit that from where we stand here on Earth, we just don't know.

A family outing, somewhere in the cosmos. Of the billions upon billions of stars in the Universe, shouldn't at least a few million support planets with intelligent life?

Fact File: Encountering UFOs

People report encountering UFOs in many ways. One astronomer, J. Allen Hynek, studied these ways and came up with these basic types of UFO encounters: distant sightings and close encounters.

In a distant sighting, a UFO appears too far away for anyone to figure out what it might really be or describe it in detail. But when people report UFO encounters at <u>close</u> range, we call them close encounters. Hynek said there are three kinds of close encounters:

1. Close Encounters of the First Kind: Sighting UFOs at Close Range

Most people who encounter UFOs only see them. In this kind of encounter, the UFOs do not leave any evidence of having been where people see them. Many people describe the UFO in detail. But even this kind of close encounter is rare.

In this illustration, a UFO hovers over a ship at sea. It is close enough to be sighted, reported, and even photographed by people on board the ship. But it has left no physical evidence. Indeed, many people will doubt even photographic evidence of this kind of encounter.

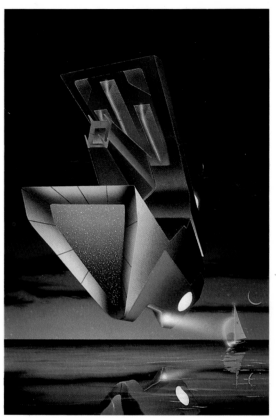

2. Close Encounters of the Second Kind: Physical Evidence or Effects From UFOs

Some people report that UFOs they have encountered leave some kind of physical evidence, like marks on the ground. Or they sometimes say that they felt sick or that the UFOs brought strange smells or sensations such as static electricity, strong magnetism, and heat.

In this photograph, four people examine a presumed UFO landing site near Richmond, Virginia, on April 21, 1967. Most evidence of this sort is eventually found to be left by something far less exciting than a flying saucer!

28

3. Close Encounters of the Third Kind: Sighting or Contacting Beings In or Around UFOs

When people report seeing, contacting, or feeling the presence of beings in or near UFOs, Hynek said they are reporting Close Encounters of the Third Kind. (This is how the popular movie about a make-believe Earth encounter with beings from UFOs got its name!)

This kind of encounter, of course, is the most famous. But it's not always the kind that most people will take seriously. This painting illustrates one man's claim to have been taken up by a saucer like craft to a giant "mother ship" high above Earth. There, he claims to have met with handsome humanoids from Venus.

What Should You Do If You Encounter a UFO?

- First, don't panic.

- Remember that "UFO" means just that — <u>unidentified</u> flying object. "Unidentified" only means that you don't know what it is. Most things people think of as UFOs really <u>can</u> be identified after checking.

- People often see bright stars, planets, comets, meteors, satellites, airplanes, and even birds — but think that they are something else. Sometimes, unusual weather conditions make ordinary things in the sky look unusual. So remember that a UFO is probably nothing to be frightened about. It's just something that you can't identify — at least when you first see it.

- If you can, just ask someone else — maybe a parent, teacher, or older relative — to look at the UFO with you. Chances are that they can tell you what it <u>really</u> is!

- Sometimes, newspapers and television and radio news programs can tell you what a UFO really was. When a satellite falls or when a meteor shower happens, it becomes news!

- If you try to find out about a UFO and still don't know after checking, ask your parents or teachers for more help. You might also want to ask a science teacher, or even a professor at a university or college near you, about what it really might have been. Sometimes, people at a museum or planetarium might be able to tell you what a UFO really was.

More Books About Unidentified Flying Objects

Here are more books that are about unidentified flying objects or contain information about UFOs. If you are interested in them, check your library or bookstore.

Creatures from UFOs. Cohen (Archway)
Is There Life on Other Planets? Asimov (Gareth Stevens)
Monsters, Mysteries, UFOs. Spellman (Learning Works)
Nancy Drew: Flying Saucer Mystery. Keene (Wanderer Books)
UFO. Blumberg (Avon)
UFO Encounters. Gelman & Seligson (Scholastic)
A UFO Has Landed. Dank & Dank (Dell)
Unidentified Flying Objects. Collins (Raintree)

For More Information About UFOs

Many organizations are interested in giving or receiving information about unidentified flying objects and other unusual, unexplained phenomena. Here are some that you can write to or call. Be sure to tell them exactly what you want to know about or report. When writing, remember to include your age, full name, and address.

For UFO news updates or other information about UFOs:
Skeptical Inquirer
Committee for the Scientific Investigation of Claims of the Paranormal (CSICP)
Box 229
Central Park Station
Buffalo, New York 14215

J. Allen Hynek Center for UFO Studies (CUFOS)
2457 W. Peterson
Chicago, Illinois 60659

To Report a UFO Sighting:
UFO Reporting Center
24-hour telephone
(206) 722-3000

Glossary

abduct: to take someone away against his or her will.

alien: in this book, a being from some place other than Earth.

ball lightning: an unusual form of lightning that is ball-shaped.

billion: in this book, the number represented by 1 followed by nine zeroes — 1,000,000,000. In some places, such as the United Kingdom (Britain), this number is called "a thousand million." In these places, one billion would then be represented by 1 followed by *12* zeroes — 1,000,000,000,000: a million million, known as a trillion in North America.

Close Encounters of the First Kind: UFO sightings at close range, according to a system developed by astronomer J. Allen Hynek. In this kind of sighting, other than the stories people tell of having seen them nearby, no actual physical evidence of an encounter with UFOs exists.

Close Encounters of the Second Kind: encounters with UFOs in which some kind of physical evidence or effects of a UFO exist.

Close Encounters of the Third Kind: encounters with UFOs in which people report seeing, physically contacting, or feeling the presence of beings in or near a UFO.

comet: an object made of ice, rock, and gas which has a vapor tail that may be seen when the comet's orbit is close to the Sun.

developer: in this book, a chemical used to bring out the image on exposed photographic film. Developer can also be used to change the image to create misleading results.

fad: an activity or fashion that quickly becomes very popular but usually for a very short time.

galaxy: a large grouping of stars, gas, and dust that exists in the Universe. Our Galaxy is known as the Milky Way.

hoax: an act which is intended to deceive and which is later proven to be trickery.

humanoid: resembling a human in appearance or having human features.

light-year: the distance traveled by light in one year, nearly six trillion miles (9.6 trillion km).

meteor: A meteoroid, or lump of rock or metals that has entered Earth's atmosphere. Also, the bright streak of light made as the meteroid enters or moves through the atmosphere.

mirage: an image that appears real but is not.

negative: in this book, a piece of photographic film that is used to produce a photograph.

phenomena: plural of **phenomenon**, which is any happening or fact in the Universe.

pyramids: enormous structures built by the ancient Egyptians in about 2500 BC. One pyramid may consist of as many as 2,300,000 blocks of stone.

skeptic: someone who disbelieves, doubts, or questions beliefs that others generally feel are true.

UFO: the abbreviation for Unidentified Flying Object.

vehicles: machines that move which can be used to transport people and materials.

Venus: a planet in our Solar system, the second planet from the Sun.

will o' the wisp: shifting, glowing light over swampy areas caused by methane, a gas that can catch fire.

Index

The publishers wish to thank the following for permission to reproduce copyright material: front cover, pp. 11, 14 (lower left), 16-17, © Julian Baum, 1988; pp. 4-5, © Mark Maxwell, 1988; pp. 5 (lower right), 7, 8-9, 23, 29, © David A. Hardy; pp. 6, 17 (lower right), photograph courtesy of Julian Baum; p. 9 (both), © Gary Milburn/Tom Stack and Associates; pp. 10 (both), 12-13, 17 (upper right), 18-19 (all), 20 (both), 22 (lower), 28, Fortean Picture Library; p. 14 (upper left), Buff Corsi/Tom Stack and Associates; p. 14 (lower right), National Severe Storms Laboratory; pp. 14-15, courtesy of NASA; p. 21 (all), © Don Schmitt/Center for UFO Studies; p. 22, Center for UFO Studies; p. 24 (both), *Sun*; p. 25 (upper right and upper left), *National Examiner*; p. 25 (middle left and lower left), *Weekly World News*; p. 26, © MariLynn Flynn, 1988; p. 28, © Mark Dowman.